SOMETIMES I NEED TO BE HUGGED
PSALM 84 FOR CHILDREN

BY ELSPETH CAMPBELL MURPHY
ILLUSTRATED BY JANE E. NELSON

SOMETIMES I NEED TO BE HUGGED
PSALM 84 FOR CHILDREN

BY ELSPETH CAMPBELL MURPHY
ILLUSTRATED BY JANE E. NELSON

NOTE: Psalm 84 is attributed to the "Sons of Korah" rather than to David. The Sons of Korah belonged to the priestly tribe of Levi, and served as Tabernacle doorkeepers and later as Temple musicians.

4

You know what, God?

Today I saw a sparrow flying to the top of our house with a caterpillar in her beak.

Dad says there's a nest up there for her babies.

I can hear the babies chirping. They sound as if they're saying,
  "Mommy, mommy, mommy!"
  "Daddy, daddy, daddy!"
They open their mouths as wide as they can, and their mommy and daddy drop the food inside.

And at night, when it's dark outside, the baby sparrows snuggle down in the nest under their parents' warm, soft wings and go to sleep.

You know what, God? Baby sparrows need to be hugged.

9

I know, because sometimes I need to be hugged, too.
Especially when things don't go so well.

This morning I was sure my best friend would be over the measles so he could walk to school with me. But he wasn't.

12

13

14

And I was sure the teacher would pick me for "Helper of the Day."
But she didn't.
And I didn't think I would spill a whole jar of paint.
But I did.

I told mom all about it when I got home.

She put her arms around me and said, "Cheer up, honey. Tomorrow's another day."

Suddenly I didn't feel so tired anymore, and I knew everything was going to be all right.

And that's the way I feel when I remember how much you love me.

For you are my God.
You give me strength when I'm sad and tired.
You're as soothing as rain on a hot, dusty day.

I'd rather have one day with you than a thousand days without you.

I'd rather hold open a door for someone—like for my dad, when he's got too much to carry—than show off by doing something that makes you sad.

For you are my God.
Your love cheers me up—like the sun peeking out from behind a cloud. 23

Your love is all around me to protect me.
It makes me feel like a baby sparrow—
warm
and safe
and happy.

24